Colt Hou
The History oτ
W H Colt Son & Company Ltd

H. A. Poulton
50 Fairview Court
East Grinstead
Sussex
RH19 4HD
Tel. 01342 316366

Moulton .

E G. Jan 2019

I helped a constructed my
bungalow in S. Godstone u 963
very similar to that shown on
page 29 — the Shepherds House —

The
COLT HOUSES
system

Founded

1919

COLT HOUSES
THE HISTORY OF
W H COLT SON & COMPANY LTD

Clive Kennett

Pitcairn-Knowles Publishing
Sevenoaks

Pitcairn-Knowles Publishing
Springbank House
13 Pembroke Road
Sevenoaks Kent
01959-523154
rppk@btinternet.com

Copyright W H Colt Son & Co Ltd

First published 2015

ISBN 978-0-9558591-5-1

A catalogue record for this book is available from the British Library

Printed by:
ImpressionIT
Unit 2 Maunsell Road
St Leonards-on-Sea
East Sussex TN38 9NL

01424-852116

Contents

Thanks – Acknowledgements

I must thank all those whose encouragement and suggestions finally pushed me into completing the research, writing and design of this book. Without them it would probably never have come to be published: Martin Ross, the present owner of Colts, who has allowed me free access to his records and photographs and has kindly written the foreword; Terry Tierney, for much information about the changes towards the end of the twentieth century; Desmond Waite, the architect, who has written a piece included in the Sandringham chapter; my wife, who has been very patient while I spent many hours writing and designing; Richard PK for sharing his few years of experience as an amateur publisher and his enthusiasm and John Davies, so helpful with all aspects of the printing;

And finally

This book is dedicated to Terry Tierney and Ron Thompson

Foreword

Martin Ross: Managing Director of Colt Houses.
1st October 2012 to the present day.

My building career and fascination for timber in construction began in 1982 shortly after leaving school when I joined a local building company specialising in erecting timber frame constructions which were mainly Colt pre-manufactured buildings. My role in the beginning was assisting the ground works team and putting in the infrastructure for the timber buildings to be erected on. As time went by and my knowledge and experience increased, I was soon assisting the carpenters with erecting the buildings in their entirety!

During my time working with Colt products, I have had the privilege of working on many prestigious projects including the Queen's Estate at Sandringham, the construction of a new bungalow in Jersey and the re-shingling of a roof on an early Colt house in Southern Ireland to name but a few.

Although the building company was independent of Colt Houses, the work they carried out was solely on Colt buildings. When the owner of the company, Mr Terry Tierney, was offered the chance to take over W.H.Colt Son & Company Limited in 1996, he along with his employees, made the transition to the new company and continued to manufacture and supply quality buildings. The Company moved to new premises in 1998 and had 14 good years improving the brand of Colt Houses. During this time I fulfilled the role of Site Manager taking responsibility for the day to day running of the on-site building work.

In 2012 Terry Tierney decided he would retire from the company and offered me the opportunity to take over as the new owner in the same way as he had done. After more than a quarter of a century as an employee, I was very honoured. In October 2012, along with my wife, Caroline, we became the new owners of Colt Houses.

It had always appealed to Terry to document the history of Colts Houses, but with the pressures of running a busy company, the time was never there to achieve it. In 2009, with the dedication of Terry's office assistant, Clive Kennett, the author of Colt Houses, and the historical knowledge of Colt's long serving draughtsman, Ronald Thompson, the documentation and information started to come together; the history of Colt Houses, and Terry's vision, was starting to become a reality. Ron's contribution to the company since 1967 has been unprecedented and to this day he remains a firm friend of both Terry and myself.

Unfortunately, with Terry's retirement and my settling into my new role, writing the history of Colt Houses was put on hold. Two years later, in the spring of 2014, I decided to contact Clive Kennett to ask him to assist with finishing his work so that the many Colt home owners and others with an interest in timber-frame buildings could appreciate it. His response was positive and encouraging.

Following my long association with the company I am pleased to see this important story told, and would like to stress the importance of the positions of Terry Tierney and Ronald Thompson in the development of Colt. The near century of evolution from the supply of hen houses to the provision of comfortable homes, as well as commercial buildings on Royal Estates, is described in detail by Clive Kennett in this excellent account of the history of Colt Houses, which every owner of a Colt home will appreciate.

Introduction

Colt Homes use less energy than conventionally built homes in both the running and the building. Materials used come from managed renewable resources. Building a Timber frame home saves around 4 tonnes of CO_2 being released into the atmosphere in comparison to a house using the more traditional brick and block method which remains popular in England. Colt houses use less energy to heat as they retain their heat and they stay cool in summer. Across the world over 70% of houses are made using the timber frame method but in England the figure is nearer 15%.

If you are living in a Colt home, you will probably be aware of many of these facts. However the Colt house has more of a story to tell…

A modern Colt home

Embossed paper stamp from the early days

The Company And Its Beginings - 1919 to 1930

The original company— W H Colt— was founded in 1919, just after World War I, by William Gleischner. He had learnt the skill of carpentry when he was confined in Wales as a German national living in the UK during the First World War. He was born in 1888 and in 1911 had married Libby Colt whose name he took. They settled in Kent. He put his skills to use by building poultry houses in a workshop in Bethersden.

Colt was initially an inventor and designed the ventilation system used in the poultry houses which were of high quality. They were designed in such a way that they remained ventilated whichever way the wind was blowing.

These poultry houses were not just sheds for chickens; they were designed to give ventilation to the birds which kept them healthy and disease free. One of the main principles was that the buildings were not ventilated through the roof but through the specially designed vents. Windows were deemed as *"purely auxiliary"* and could be kept closed during bad weather but the poultry houses still remained ventilated. In the words used in the W H Colt catalogue -

Extensible Unit Building
Super Houses for Super Hens

> *"There is no accumulation of spent and odorous air,*
> *even when windows and doors have to be kept shut dur-*
> *ing long spells of inclement weather"*

The catalogue also contains many endorsements from satisfied customers, including one from Major W. Hayland Wilson telling Mr Colt that housing his birds in a Colt poultry shed had dramatically reduced mortality in his flock and increased egg production. This letter was dated 9th January 1924 and was one of many offering such endorsements and recommendation.

Manufacture of the poultry houses, some of them very large commercial units, continued alongside the manufacture of the houses for many years. Such was Mr Colt's knowledge and expertise on the well-being of poultry in relation to their housing

Commercial chicken housing manufactured by Colt shown on a farm in Rickmansworth Herts sometime in the 1920s

Shows 4 units = 20' × 15'. 2 outside sections with inside nests. 2 inner sections with outside nests.
Observe floorlights front and back.
Fitted with steel sashes and oval guttering.
From £47 10s. complete, according to height and accessories.
This house is erected on oak stakes 2ft. off ground, which is heavy clay soil.
The house may also be placed on low foundations.

From an early catalogue

that he travelled the country giving talks to poultry societies on the virtues of correctly ventilating poultry housing.

Another Colt innovation - The Monorail Poultry House or Track Ranger as it was advertised, enabled the house to be moved and thus help to rotate and share grazing with other livestock. The smaller units were supplied with a single removable rail in the centre, with wheels on the underside of the poultry house. Larger houses would have two rails.

How the transition came about from the manufacture of poultry houses to the production of complete houses is not too certain. It

Colts Monorail or Track Ranger Poultry House made moving the poultry easy—taken from an early catalogue

Still in existence—spotted in Hampshire a Colt Track Ranger without its rail

has been said that one of the early Colt customers was so impressed with the quality of their poultry house that they converted it into holiday accommodation. However an early design of poultry house which was designed to house incubators for hatching chicks, was made with a higher insulation value and also included accommodation for the poultry man. This could have inspired Mr Colt to branch out into the luxury house market.

Further clues to this transition can be found in an extract from an early version of a company brochure for "Extensible Unit Buildings". This is written in very formal English seldom encountered in modern brochures:

"The manufacturers of the Extensible Unit Buildings
have had considerable experience of both the manu-
facturing and the marketing of small wooden buildings.

Although we have not hitherto put our hand to residential buildings, except to execute a few special orders outside our usual routine, we have been so constantly approached, almost besieged on the subject, that we have felt for some time we might usefully make an attempt to relieve the present unfortunate situation.

We feel that we possess the essential qualities for work of this kind: ability to carry out the manufacturing and knowledge, through close contact with the public, of what is wanted.

We therefore embark, after very careful deliberation and preparation, with a definite policy.

We are putting on the market small wooden houses which will be inexpensive, durable, easily erected, and have some pretence to elegance and design.

Their cost is so low that no one will hesitate to buy one for a temporary dwelling, and yet they will be so strong and compact that they will recommend themselves to many as permanent houses."

The company's use of the word "extensible" is interesting as the word has today faded from general use. There is a subtle difference between this word and the more commonly used "extendable" which may well refer to a brush handle or something that can be extended at the push of a button. Extensible means that the ability to extend at a later date was designed into the buildings. The word today is mainly associated with computer software and is used by developers to describe computer software that has a built-in life extendibility to cope with future changes in computer hardware and operating systems. This extendibility must be what Colt had in mind as, even today, Colt homes can be easily extended and adapted to suit the changing requirements of the occupants.

For whatever reason, the company had started manufacture of homes as well as poultry houses and, once this idea was established, Colt travelled to America where he was impressed with the timber framed homes he saw built with cedar wood cladding and cedar tiles.

The company had started house manufacture when William Colt met Jack O'Hea who was impressed by the products Colt offered. The company's fortunes took a turn for the better when, in 1925, William Colt and Jack O'Hea became partners. The office of the company which was formed by the pair - W H Colt (London) Ltd - was located in Bush House in the Strand in London which, until recently, was also home to the BBC World Service. Some catalogues from the twenties also give a Belfast address as an office of the company. With Jack's skills in marketing and publicity he helped to increase the profile of the company and its products with some innovative publicity.

Amongst a number of publicity schemes, the company ran high profile advertising in the national press and attended the Daily Mail Ideal Home exhibition.

Maximum publicity was obtained when Jack O'Hea persuaded HRH the Prince of Wales to perform an opening ceremony on a Miners' Cottage which was one of the Colt designs and which had been erected on some vacant land adjacent to Bush House where subsequently other demonstration homes were erected.   The prince had become interested in the cottage when he became involved in the plight of the miners who, in the nineteen twenties, were enduring considerable hardship.

Following interest by the Prince, other famous names visited the show house over subsequent weeks. One such personality was a Lady Asquith, a socialite of the time, who Jack had collected and driven to the site. These events thus further increased the profile of the cottage, its method of construction and the company.

Workers look on as HRH the Prince of Wales is shown around the
Colt Miners' Cottage

The Prince of Wales was interested enough to purchase a number of these cottages. The National Council of Social Service under The Miners Transfer Scheme also purchased these houses after HRH had mentioned how wonderfully low the price was and how much nicer it looked than the average bungalow. This was backed up by the many letters received by the company from the Duchy of Cornwall and other occupiers of such houses extolling the virtues of the levels of comfort and good appearance of the houses as well as their resistance to weather.

It was during this time that the company introduced the use of Western Red cedar shingles for the roofing of the houses built by W H Colt. The company became the first to commercially import these into Britain from Canada and formed Colt Building Products Limited to sell the shingles commercially in the UK. These attractive roof tiles have been used on thousands of buildings across the country and are still used today on modern Colt homes.

Jack O'Hea and the Prince outside the Miners' Cottage

The main method of construction during this early period was by using modular panels. The idea was that the buildings were produced using a modular 4 foot (1219mm) panel which meant that customers could purchase an "extensible" building to whatever size suited their means. The panels could be manufactured as components in greater quantities which helped with production and kept costs down. For the extensible poultry houses, the panels were clad externally, also meaning less time on site constructing the units.

In these early days the concept of timber meant that the provision of a complete house clearly had an economic advantage over more conventionally built houses at the time. This advantage was shown in a catalogue issued by the company at an early stage showing the "100 Guinea House". This was a very basic single storey residence. An idea of how basic comes in the description of the

The demonstration house is dwarfed by the buildings of Aldwych in London

"Kent" Bungalow size No 1 that consists of a living room, kitchen and two bedrooms. The catalogue goes on to say:

> " The arrangement of the rooms shown in the plans may be altered so as to provide for the inclusion of a bath, W.C., larder, etc, according to individual needs, by additional partitions and doors...."

Clearly some individuals did not require a bathroom, probably because of the tradition of bathing in a tub in the living room. Toilets were at this time commonly at the bottom of the garden. On the other end of the scale however the company was supplying some very grand residences indeed. In order to attract both ends of the market, the catalogue suggested that the 100 Guinea house could be used for a permanent home or a holiday residence.

By the end of the twenties, W H Colt Ltd had become an established manufacturer and supplier of poultry houses, homes and furniture. This was due no doubt to William Colt's innovative approach to manufacturing the homes, coupled with Jack O'Hea's flare for marketing and publicity.

The sales literature from the 100 Guinea House Brochure

10

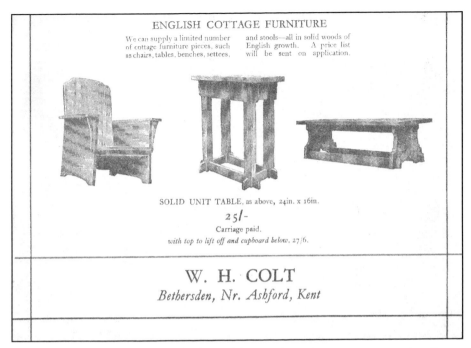

Also shown in the 100 Guinea House brochure was a selection
of the furniture which Colt was manufacturing

By this time the company was producing many houses designed
by many different architects and had gained a reputation as a supplier of quality homes. It was supplying not only some very grand
designs but also continued to supply to the lower end of the market
with the Miners' Cottage, and similar designs. In the eleven years
in existence the business had diversified from producing poultry
houses to covering a wide range of requirements for timber buildings. This included introducing the idea that timber could supply a
complete solution to housing requirements. In respect of timber
homes, they were creating their market rather than just supplying
poultry houses where the market already existed. They had become an established importer of Western Red shingles from Canada. In addition to this, other building and ventilation products were
also being introduced; once again, this was driven by Jack O'Hea.

Manufacturing continued in Bethersden where it remained for many years to come. The office in London was also maintained as a main sales office. The vacant land adjacent to Bush House continued to be used for demonstration buildings.

Publicity 1930 - 1940

During the thirties, the company built its reputation as a supplier of quality houses and became known much more for its homes than its poultry houses. New standard house designs were being introduced and shown in numerous catalogues which the company produced during this period. It also undertook bespoke projects. The houses were stylish and typified the house type generally built in the years up to the Second World War.

The projects became more ambitious and an example of this is an old people's home in Leningrad which was designed during the early thirties. The building, which was called, "Hostel for Infirm British Subjects in Russia", was designed by Professor Abercrombie and some detail appeared in a catalogue in about 1931. Professor Abercrombie produced not only a drawing, which remains in the company archives, but also had a model made, and pictures of the model are also shown in the Colt catalogue. It is not clear from the records whether this project actually went ahead. Following World War II, Abercrombie became involved in ambitious plans to rebuild London after the Blitz but these were never carried out.

Professor Abercrombie's Design for
HOSTEL FOR INFIRM BRITISH SUBJECTS in Russia.
To be manufactured in England by W. H. COLT, LTD., and erected by them near Leningrad.

Showing how the Hostel will look when completed. Photograph of a model made from Professor Abercrombie's plans.
This should be compared with the drawing of the layout given overleaf.

A picture of the model of Professor Abercrombie's design for the old peoples home in Leningrad — from a Colt Catalogue

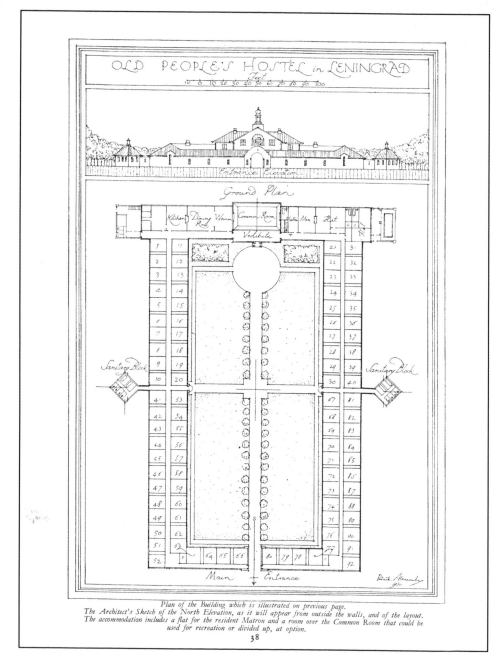

OLD PEOPLE'S HOSTEL in LENINGRAD

Feet

Entrance Elevation

Ground Plan

Kitchen | Dining Rm | Women | Common Room | Matron | Men | Flat

Vestibule

Sanitary Block

Sanitary Block

Main ╪ Entrance

Plan of the Building which is illustrated on previous page.
*The Architect's Sketch of the North Elevation, as it will appear from outside the walls, and of the layout.
The accommodation includes a flat for the resident Matron and a room over the Common Room that could be
used for recreation or divided up, at option.*

38

Professor Abercrombie's grand design for a home for the British Infirm in
Russia

Looking along an outside wall of the enclosure.

Another view of Professor Abercrombie's model

To accommodate these larger projects, manufacture and construction methods changed. Generally during this time houses were "stick built". This method involved the individual panels being built on site from scratch using the timber delivered to site in random lengths. This was a departure from the modular approach used for the poultry house although that method was re-introduced much later on.

The company was a regular exhibitor at the Daily Mail Ideal Homes exhibition and often displayed complete houses at the show. Some of these houses were purchased directly at the show and re-erected on the customers' own plots.

During the partnership between Jack O'Hea and William Colt, Jack had introduced other products and attempted various forms of diversification and the company had grown steadily, no doubt largely down to Jack's work in publicising the products. In 1931 however the two partners decided to go their separate ways. Jack O'Hea took all aspects of the business apart from the timber buildings and went on to form Colt International, a multi-national company which specialised in various forms of ventilation and associated products. The Colt International headquarters is today in Havant in Hampshire and members of Jack O'Hea's family remain involved. Both companies continue to use the Colt name. As part of the agreement, Jack O'Hea also took Colt Building Products Ltd who imported the cedar shingles. Today this trades as The Loft Shop and still sells a product called Colt Preceda shingles.

Although the office in Bush House remained until the building was requisitioned during World War II, William Colt continued to manufacture timber buildings in the factory at Bethersden under the name of W H Colt Son & Co Ltd which remains as the registered name today. The company did, however, take a London office off Trafalgar Square after leaving Bush House. It was in Bethersden also that demonstration houses were erected for prospective customers to inspect.

The Colts had a son, born in 1911, who was named Charles Frank but for some unknown reason always went by the name of Michael or Mick. He studied architecture under Sir Albert Richardson during the thirties. In the company archives there are many drawings by Michael Colt which show him to be a talented designer, even at an early age, although he didn't contribute many house designs for the company to sell which was generally left to architectural practices. The following page, however, shows a large house attributed to Michael. Sir Albert Richardson himself later designed a recreation hall using Colt components for the Long John Distillery in Scotland and was one of many architects who became involved with Colt.

As the company began to increase the manufacture of homes, standard designs were introduced for customers to browse and select. These designs were published in the Colt catalogues. The company would always be willing to adapt the basic designs to suit customers needs and in reality, the standard designs were rarely built. Although the company supplied fairly small cottages, most of the designs in their catalogues tended to be quite grand country house designs. The ranges of designs were often given names, also rather grand, which related to times or events. Examples are The Coronation, The Empire, The Festival and The Regency. The Empire was so named because of the rapid transport links to Canada, part of the British Empire, and where so much of the materials for the houses were sourced.

Although Colt advertised their cedar houses with cedar cladding and shingles, it was also possible to clad the houses with the more conventional brick elevations and clay tile roofs.

It is interesting to note also that many of the houses on show in the thirties still had servants quarters or at least a maid's bedroom. Alongside one design however it states:

> *"Many people who wish to run a small house without a resident maid will find it a great convenience to have one large living room adjoining a compact and well planned kitchen ..."*

Architect, C. F. Col

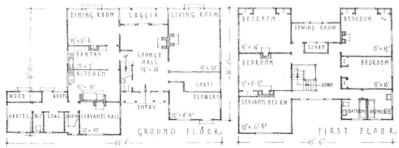

This five- or six-bedroom house was built for a client in the Heythrop Hunt at Heythrop, near Chipping Norton, Oxfordshire. The outside has been painted a light cream, contrasting well with the cedar tiling on the roof, the trim being a special tint of green. Being on a very high and exposed site, the outside boarding is double, i.e. Columbian pine under-boarding and red cedar outside. In addition to stabling, three cottages close by have been erected to accommodate groom, house and garden staff. All these have been left in the natural cedar colour of russet brown, weathering grey. Illustrations of the latter on application.

Michael's name is found against some grand house designs, including the one shown in this early extract from the Homes & Gardens Magazine

A 1939 catalogue published a price list which gives the approximate price of a two storey cottage (Type MP106) as £675 to £700 "All In". All in means that the house is ready for occupation. A separate approximate price for the "superstructure" only delivered to site for the same house is given as £275. Customers are informed that they are charged a nominal fee of £5.5s.0d (£5.25) for *"the services of preparation of drawings to the number required by the various authorities concerned (Local, Town Planning, etc)"*

The Catalogues also warn prospective customers of the copyright laws in relation to the house designs. The catalogue also states:

"ALL COMMUNICATIONS should be addressed to the firm direct and it is important to note that no travellers are employed"

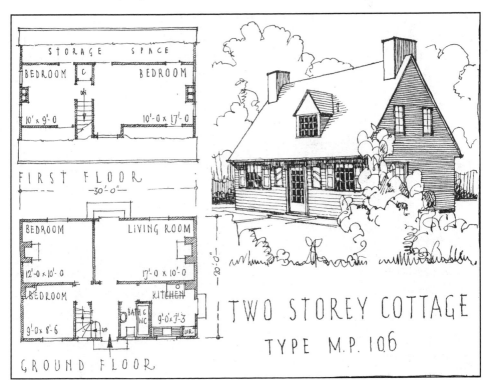

The Two Storey Cottage – Type M.P. 106

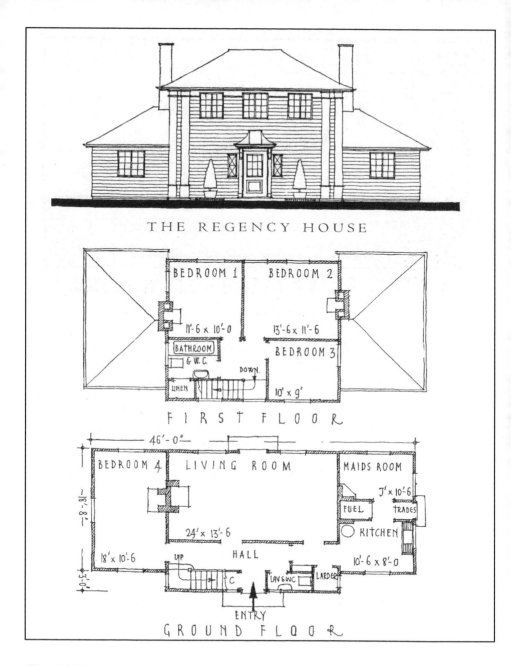

THE REGENCY HOUSE

FIRST FLOOR

BEDROOM 1
11'-6 x 10'-0

BEDROOM 2
13'-6 x 11'-6

BATHROOM & W.C.

BEDROOM 3
10' x 9'

LINEN

DOWN.

GROUND FLOOR

46'-0"

18'-8"

3'-0"

BEDROOM 4
18' x 10'-6

LIVING ROOM
24' x 13'-6

MAIDS ROOM
7' x 10'-6

FUEL

TRADES

KITCHEN
10'-6 x 8'-0

HALL

UP

C

LAV & WC

LARDER

ENTRY

The 1939 catalogue also lists the approximate price of the much grander Regency House as £1200 "All in" with a superstructure only price of £350

The company was therefore quite sensitive about the use of their designs but states that it is possible for a customer to employ another building method subject to *"suitable terms being agreed"*.

Among the many well known architects who became involved in a specific Colt home design was Sir Edwin Lutyens and many articles featuring Colt homes appeared in Country Life Magazine over the years, including one which refers to a cedar house designed by Sir Edwin. The article dated sometime in the early 1930s and written by Randal Phillips, of Country Life, commends Colt for showing *"much discernment in seeking the best architectural advice"*. He goes on to say that Mr Colt approached the famous architect, much more widely known for his monumental works and great houses, who produced *"an admirable design"* for a timber house -

Lutyen's drawing of the house

Lutyen's drawing of the lounge and the house in recent times "*in which is displayed the same fine sense of design coupled with individuality*". The article goes on to describe the method of manufacture and erection of the house including some of the features. "*Some ground floor rooms have walls lined with cedar. Internal partitions are lined with eelgrass quilting which is sound deadening*". Eelgrass quilting was a naturally grown material which it was claimed improved sound insulation and which it was also claimed was resistant to fire although whether modern building regulations would agree, it is difficult to say. The roof is "*covered with red cedar shingles fixed in broken alignment and sweep round the valleys*".

The house was a four-bedroom house, the fourth being designated as the maid's bedroom, although the house had only one upstairs bathroom - en-suites were not in-vogue in those days. The overall gross floor area is 1414 sq ft (130 sq mts) which was a reasonable size family house.

At the end of the article Mr Randal Phillips goes into the "*all important matter of cost*" which was stated as £1315. The house was built in Chobham, Surrey and the price included "*electric wiring, drains, plumbing and sanitary fittings, fireplaces etc, internal decoration and the Aga cooker and combined dresser and hatch in the kitchen*".

Mr Phillps's final paragraph might well appear in a modern catalogue:
   " *This is a notable achievement for a well designed*
   four bedroomed house of sound construction: The
   house is ready to go into at once (since there is
   nothing to dry out) and one for which it is claimed
   that the rooms are maintained at an equable tem-
   perature at all seasons".

A L Osborne was another architect involved in the design of Colt homes; he was involved with Colt through the thirties and into the sixties; his name appears on many of the Colt drawings. He had a number of books on architectural styles published during his time.

Many splendid houses had been supplied throughout this decade but the outbreak of World War II slowed down the production with the drying up of supplies and industrial production turned to the war effort. In the twenty years since it had started, Colt had made its name in the industry.

A modern photograph of a fine example of a large country house supplied during the thirties to a site in Kent

The War Years - 1940 to 1950

Although World War II did affect the supply of houses, the company kept going and, after the war, despite short supply of materials, continued to supply houses.

Mr W H Colt continued to be involved in the business until his death in 1945 when his son Michael took over the running of the company, although Michael had always been involved in the business.

Over the years with the company, Michael Colt built houses for himself in the Weald of Kent, Ireland, Switzerland, Portugal and two in France, although these houses were built as demonstration units to assist in selling the product in the various countries.

Michael with one the Clavier Colt piano collection prior to it being shipped to Japan for an exhibition

In 1947 Michael married Lore B Lorsbach. The couple had no children. During his time with the company and apart from his involvement in the running of the business, Michael also went on to build one of the finest collections of antique pianos and harpsichords in Europe after becoming interested in the instruments. The Colt Clavier collection is still housed in Bethersden today.

Over the years Colt supplied homes to a number of celebrities and, during the early forties, the company supplied a bungalow on the estate of Sir Malcolm Campbell which was built near his main residence at Tilgate Lake near East Grinstead in Sussex.

Most of the houses sold by Colt were clad externally in timber although some were built with external brick skins or other more conventional finishes. The great majority of the houses however were clad in cedar, either cedar boarding or shingles. Below can be seen a house which was built in Thistleton in Rutland in 1949 which shows how the shingles can be fixed in various patterns rather than in just straight rows. The house shown is based on the standard KA1000 of which Colt sold many over the years. The cedar cladding and roofing is a golden brown colour when new but mellows to silver grey over the years. This house was designed by

The House in Thistleton in Rutland - Designed by A L Osborne

A L Osborne and featured in an article in "The Architect & Builder News" in 1939.

At one stage, Colt Houses became popular amongst the high ranking military officers in the British Forces. One illustration from the archives dated 1948 shows a pair of semi-detached houses which are titled, "Married Officers' Quarters" and the client's name on the drawing - the Directorate of Fortification and Works. The houses were stylish and quite grand and designed with a formal dining area and large living room, ideal for entertaining. The dining room had double doors opening on to a patio in order that the guests could spill out into the garden on a warm summers evening or on a cold winters evening, would be warmed by the installed gas or electric fire. Also with visiting dinner guests in mind, the house boasted a downstairs cloak room and toilet. Even after the war had ended, materials were in short supply and production methods changed to reflect this shortage. This is covered in greater detail later. Generally however, the company had returned to a modular approach with the manufacture of the 4 foot (1219) panel.

From the company's archives - a drawing of a pair of semi - detached houses built as officers' quarters

House designs also reflected the current economic climate as the country re-built after six years of war. There are few catalogues for this period in the company archives, but one dated 1948 warns customers that owing to the difficulties of the times they reserve the right to modify the design, construction or specification of any house during manufacture in order to maintain production. The catalogue points out some of the problems associated with lack of labour and government restrictions on the building of houses.

As the decade ended, the company was in a good position as the country entered a period of growth following the war and through the next few years was to enter its busiest period.

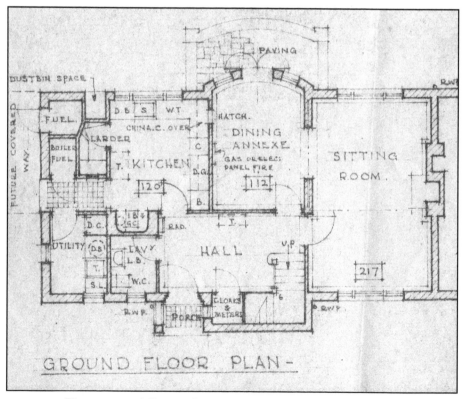

The ground floor of the married officers' quarters

Building Popularity - 1950 to 1960

During the fifties as the country began to rebuild its infrastructure following the war, Colt's business began to flourish as it ran up to its busiest period. Company records show over 1000 completed projects between 1950 and 1960.

For one such project in 1954, Colt supplied four bungalows to the Argyll Estates - The Trustees of the 10th Duke of Argyll. A photograph of one of these bungalows as it is today is shown below. Today the bungalow is part of the Auchindrain Trust and in 2009, the Trust contacted Colt to find out more about the bungalow, which has been turned into a museum. In addition, the bungalow is grade A listed. Colt were able to supply copies of the original plans for the bungalow, along with a replacement plaque which had at some time gone missing. Also supplied were some original correspondence between the company and Argyll Estates. The bungalow, originally built as a shepherds dwelling, can be visited. More information can be found at www.auchindrain-museum.org.uk.

The Shepherds House in Auchindrain – now a museum

In May 1959 the company exhibited at the Lisbon fair in Portugal and the response to the Colt products was good. Based on this, Michael Colt decided to erect a show house on a site in the hills not far from Faro. Although built as a show house, the Colts also used it as a holiday home.

According to an article which appeared in the Kent Messenger in September 1959, the whole house was loaded on to a Colt lorry and three Colt employees drove to the site where, with the help of a Portuguese labourer, the house was erected.

The land when purchased had the small round tower which was renovated as part of the project and the house butted up to the tower via a lobby. The completed house was quite small and was partly cedar clad with a cedar shingle roof. Part of the front elevation was rendered and painted white to match the tower.

Preparing for the journey to Portugal

30

The Portugal project under construction with scaffold around the tower
and below — the completed house

The right facing colt and the left facing colt

The Colt horse - technically a male horse under four years old - as seen on the company logo, has been used from the very early days and every building manufactured was supplied with a brass plaque showing the Colt horse. Originally, the plaque contained the patent numbers relating mainly to the various registered designs of poultry houses, but for the residential homes these numbers were not shown. It is interesting to note that until the early fifties, the Colt horse was on its hind legs facing the left but during the fifties this changed. The county of Kent, which uses a similar horse as part of its Invicta logo, requested that Colt should turn their horse around to face the right and the company complied. All plaques and publicity material from that point had the colt facing the other way.

Both left and right facing colts along with the Kent Invicta Colt

Busy Times - 1960 to 1970

The company continued to exhibit at exhibitions and in 1965 built a house for the Daily Mail Ideal Home exhibition where they had experienced much success over the years.

It was during the sixties and seventies the company was most active employing at one time 250 people, including 15 draughtsmen and 5 salesmen. In addition to this, the company had agents in many parts of the world selling their houses.

There were times during the late 60s to early 70s when visitors were turning up by the coach load to inspect demonstration houses at the site in Bethersden and draughtsmen and other employees were being used to help deal with the number of prospective customers who were arriving daily.

The factory at Bethersden during the sixties

Amongst the many destinations of houses over the years, 1966 saw the first Colt house delivered to the Falkland Islands. Supply of houses continued to the islands until the mid nineties. The Colt

A Colt House under construction in the Falkland Islands and below, a completed dwelling

house supplied in kit form is ideally suited to these remote locations where local building materials are in short supply and winters are harsh. For these customers, the company did not get involved with construction or erection of the houses but simply sent them in kits and local contractors on the island assembled them. The comprehensive erection instructions supplied with each kit made this easy.

In 1969 Colt supplied a school house for the Island of Tristan da Cunha in the South Atlantic. This was to be the first of a number of buildings sent to the island. These too were assembled by local people using detailed instructions supplied. A press cutting of the time reported that:

> " ...the Colt buildings were complete in every detail and included heating, plumbing and electrical equipment right down to the last nut & bolt and light bulb. The complete shipment was packed in crates up to 5cwt (250kg) each. These were lowered from

The school at Tristan da Cunha

Box Tree Cottage - Longtown in Herefordshire

The Carnarvon - a sixties style made much more attractive by the cedar cladding (designed by A. L. Osborne)

Box Tree Cottage today

the ship into long boats which were rowed ashore by the islanders."

By the sixties, the company had several houses within the UK and other parts of Europe which were used as demonstration houses. One of these, called Box Tree Cottage near Longtown on the Welsh borders, was available for employees to use as a holiday cottage. This particular house was originally a single storey stone house which was in a dilapidated state. It was Mick Colt's idea to extend upwards, thus prolonging the life of the building by protecting the ageing stonework. This once again demonstrated the adaptability of the Colt timber frame. During the Second World War, Mr & Mrs Colt lived in Box Tree Cottage and older residents of the village can remember them living in the village. This was before the first floor extension was added.

The Knole

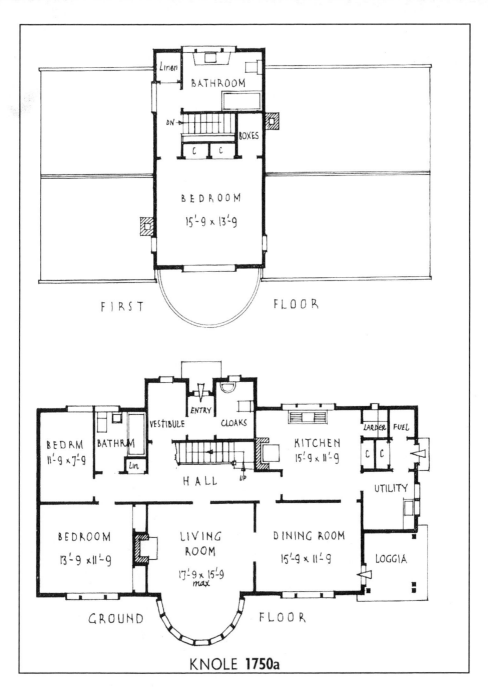

The Layout of the Knole

During the sixties, the house designs offered by the company do contain some designs synonymous with the "box" culture. The Carnarvon, (shown on a previous page), was popular amongst the customers and a good number of these were delivered during this era. A few were supplied with pitch roofs giving a slightly more conventional appearance. This house was another designed by A L Osborne.

A more stylish house shown in the 1960 catalogue is the Knole (shown on the previous page) which is described as a semi bungalow with a central two storey section, giving a third bedroom and second bathroom on the first floor. The basic design is attributed to C.P.McLaughlin L.R.I.B.A. Note also the Oriel windows which were supplied on many Colt homes.

During these busy decades, Colt continued to supply commercial as well as residential properties and in 1967 built the "Colt" public house in Ashford, Kent. Sadly, this was demolished some years ago to make way for a supermarket.

The Colt Pub

The Loch Melfort Motor Inn

Showing the versatility of the Colt system is a motel supplied at Loch Melfort, Scotland in 1966. This was a part of the conversion of the former home of the Cambells of Arduaine.

There is no doubt that Colt homes were popular during this era and in 1969, Sir John Benn wrote a letter to the Times extolling the virtues of his Colt house:

> *"I am having a six bedroom Colt house built in Surrey and although the timber superstructure was delivered only nine weeks ago, I already have a front door key in my pocket. The pride and enthusiasm of the men in this fine achievement is infectious and completely belies the idea that the British no longer do a good day's work. "*

The Loch Melfort Motor Inn

The "Do As Much As You Can" house

In an article in the June 1967 copy of "Practical Decorating & Building" the writer praises the virtues of timber frame design and build for the amateur builder or self-builder as they would be known today. The article was written following a visit by a potential self-builder to the Colt premises in Bethersden where it was demonstrated that from the early stages of design, it was possible for the potential house owner to become involved.

It was possible to chose from a wide range of standard designs or modify a design to suit individual needs. In addition to this flexibility of design, Colt bungalows have no internal load bearing walls which means that if an owner wanted to redesign the layout, it was possible.

Once the design is decided upon, the planning permission granted and an order in place for the house, it is just a case of waiting for the house to turn up on a lorry (or more than one lorry). The concrete base has to be prepared and this is one thing that it is suggested is carried out by professionals, but once the base is complete it is up to the owner to do as much or as little as he likes. It is claimed that a house can be put up by a "man and a boy equipped with scaffolding, plumb line, saws and hammers" as none of the pre-made panels are heavier than can be lifted by two people. All components are made to measure apart from random lengths of internal trims and all the panels are pre-drilled (in the right places) so with the simple to follow instructions, the house will be up in no time.

The kit can be supplied with everything down to the last detail if required, not just for individuals but for self-build groups who combine their resources by buying a plot of land and can work on the houses together and save even more money by constructing the base. There are many successful groups whose members became house owners through such schemes.

It was during 1969 that, such was the popularity of Colt Houses, the first building was manufactured and erected at the Queens Estate at Sandringham. This was to be the first of a number of buildings supplied to the estate and the supply was to continue over the next 35 years. A chapter dedicated to the Sandringham Project can be seen later in this book.

The end of the sixties had seen the busiest decade for Colt and this busy period was to continue through the seventies. The versatility of the product meant that the company was supplying not only houses but schools, village halls, golf clubs and churches, amongst many others. The Colt name had become synonymous with quality and style. From the rich and famous to the self-builder looking for their first step on the property ladder, W H Colt was able to service their needs.

BUILDING BY NUMBERS

1: Foundations, footings and oversite concreting is much the same as for a bricks and mortar house. Build chimney stack, if required, to first floor level.

2: Complete timber house 'kit' arrives on site in one or more 15 ton lorries. Average price for a three bedroom house for a level site close to mains supplies such as this is approximately £2,200, but if built entirely by professional labour costs rise to nearer £5,500.

3: Building by numbers means that a number is printed on every component and all numbers are identified on the working plans. When this is not practical full assembly instructions are printed on the parts themselves in positions where they will not show when the house is completed. Wall panels are ready battened for attaching the external cedar cladding. Colt claim that their houses can be put up by 'a man and a boy', equipped with scaffolding, plumb line, saws and hammers.

4&5: Roof level is reached. All parts are scaled so that they can be propped, lifted or manhandled by one person. In this design the roof trusses also form the second storey.

6 & 7: The last wall panels are attached to the dormer window gable end. All wall panels are bolted together, reinforced

by rust resistant alloy nails which are also used for attaching external cladding.

8: Cedar board cladding arrives in random lengths for cutting to size on site.

9: Tiling battens are nailed across the rafters for fixing the cedar shingles. These can be left to mellow to a silver grey colour or treated with a special oil dressing to preserve their original shade. Either way the shingles last for the full life of the house.

10: Fixing the PVC rainwater goods included in the kit.

11: The cladding almost completed.

12: The natural colour variations in the cladding boards can be exploited for interesting effects, as seen on the cheeks of the dormer window.

13: With the windows glazed, the house is complete. Glass is not included in the price of the kit.

Part of the article "The Do As Much As You Can" house reproduced by kind permission of Practical Decorating and Building based on the building of a Colt home.

The Peak Years - 1970 to 1980

The popularity of Colt continued into the seventies with many types of houses and commercial buildings being supplied to many parts of the country and some to other parts of the world. This was in the heyday of the company and during its busiest times as many as three houses a day were leaving the factory in Bethersden. The company continued to use their basic design catalogue whilst modifying these designs to suit customer's individual needs. They had a number of demonstration houses at the site in Bethersden and in other parts of Europe where potential customers were able to see for themselves what could be achieved.

Into the seventies, the designs became a little more stylish after the utility sixties. The following design is based on the "New England", although the white pvc cladding to the lower elevation is somewhat uncharacteristic. Metal Crittal windows were typical during this era and standard issue on Colt Houses.

The New England

The Crawley Self-Build Project

Colt houses continued to be popular with self-build groups who collectively purchased land and built a number of houses using largely their own labour. The Colt "kit" house lends itself to this system rather well. The self-build system enabled people who otherwise would not have been able to afford a new house, the chance to do so. The photo above shows one such project in Crawley, West Sussex. As each house was completed, it was common in these projects for the participants, who were often tradesmen, to draw straws as to who would occupy the first house.

As the company endeavoured to sell into other parts of Europe, demonstration houses were added and the following picture shows one such house which was built near Strasbourg. Like their other overseas houses, this one doubled as a holiday cottage for Mr & Mrs Colt.

A House in the Alsace

It wasn't only for the individual that the company was supplying houses, but increasingly, village halls, churches, sports club houses, schools and even office blocks. Such was the popularity of the construction method. This also signalled a general and subtle change in the type of buildings which the company were supplying. This change was to take place over the next ten years. At this time however, the beginnings of the environmental movement had started to make its voice heard and the energy efficient credentials of the timber frame house were being recognised as a desirable aspect of owning a home. Even though at this time, the houses were not particularly well insulated, the environmental impact of building the houses was known to be low and their insulation values exceeded the requirements of the building regulations at the time. New timber frame companies began to appear, although at this time largely catering for the individual and self-build market, the system had not yet started to be used by the developers. It was going to be another ten years before the requirements for energy conservation and the need for speedy construction would see the large developers using the timber frame system.

From the early days of Colt, the company had prided itself on supplying a "turnkey" package – a house that you could move straight into. The houses were complete to the last detail. To handle the complete build, a separate company had been formed called Cedar Construction which carried out all the ancillary work from foundations to the final coat of paint. Colt manufactured the timber frame and Cedar Construction erected it and did all of the site work.

Towards the end of the seventies however, Colt was concentrating more on production of houses and Cedar Construction was carrying out less building work. Colt started to use sub-contract companies to carry out this work. This may also have been a move to help to compete with new companies who specialised in the manufacture and supply of the structural element of the house and leaving the rest of the work to project managers or builders.

Colt was an important part of Bethersden and the local economy, being by far the largest employer in what is generally a rural and non industrial area.

Commercial Buildings - 1980 to 1990

Michael Colt ran the company and was involved until his death in 1985. He was, according to the employees who worked with him, a very strict authoritarian in his day to day dealings, although he would treat the employees to a day trip to France for an annual outing. During his time he was passionate about the company's products and would enthuse about their benefits. Although not actively involved in the running of the company, he insisted on signing off all drawings. Mrs Colt was also a frequent visitor to the factory.

The company was carrying out more larger scale projects and less houses but despite a general dropping off of orders, customers continued to come to Colt from all parts of the world and in 1980 a house was delivered to the Gambia for Mr Edgar. This house was shipped to Gambia and erected by sub-contractors with the help of the locals although a Colt employee was sent to supervise the construction of the main frame of the house. This house was located next door to the presidential palace in Gambia.

In the late eighties, Colt supplied the new pavilion for the Kent County Agricultural Society at Detling. The building work was carried out by Tierney Construction whose owner, Terry Tierney was later to take over Colt. The completed pavilion was opened by The Queen on her first visit to the Kent County Show in July 1989.

Another prestigious project which was carried out in 1987 was the building of Sandford Springs Golf Club in Wolverton, Hampshire.

Following Michael's death, the company saw a decline in its business although this was not necessarily linked. Changes in the market and competition from new timber frame companies using new efficient techniques were able to appeal to a wider market. This coupled with aggressive marketing techniques being used by these new companies was to affect and reduce W H Colts share of the market. The Colt method of construction had perhaps not moved with the times. Also, the idea of a wooden house had fallen out of fashion to a certain extent, although timber frame houses, with more traditional brick or render exteriors were being built in greater numbers. This was true for both the individual builders which W H Colt had served so well in the past, and developers who had started using timber frame to reduce construction times and improve insulation values.

Another factor affecting the company was the low availability of building plots in rural areas which had been Colts mainstay for many years. These plots were becoming a rarity and if they were available, were becoming too expensive to make building an individual house economic. Over the years many Colt houses had been built on rural plots, often quite secluded, but affordable plots which were available in the late eighties were in areas where the planners would be reluctant to allow a dwelling clad in timber.

Mick relaxing during a Colt Day out

Kent County Showground pavillion at Detling supplied by W H Colt in 1989 and opened by HM the Queen, as it is today

Sandford Springs Club House main entrance and two years after the completion of the original building, a rotunda was added to the rear of the club house. Construction work on the rotunda is shown below

The completed rotunda

In addition to these factors the economic climate and the general downturn in the construction industry at the time was also to affect the company's fortune. While the company continued to win some impressive contracts, house building was declining and no longer their main activity.

After many years of having an enviable position as a market leader in the timber house industry, this decade saw the start of a general decline in the company's fortunes as its markets began to change.

Sandringham - The Thirty Five Year Royal Project

In 1969, Colt supplied and erected their first building on the Royal Estate at Sandringham. The cafeteria, which was a modified standard Colt bungalow, was clad in cedar. This was the first of a number of Colt buildings to be supplied and erected on the Royal site. The building housed a kitchen and serving area alongside an area selling souvenirs. The following photo was extracted from the pages of a local paper at the time.

As the Sandringham Estate grew in popularity with public visitors, several expansion projects took place over the next 35 years.

Two years after the cafeteria, W H Colt supplied a flower stall, although when originally supplied it was an ice cream kiosk. The kiosk was octagonal and based on ten of the standard Colt four-

The original cafeteria being built in 1969

The visitor centre flower stall/ice cream parlour

foot panels fitted between specially made stanchions.

In 1974 a souvenir shop was built to allow more space to be used in the cafeteria where originally the country park souvenirs were sold. This was partly timber clad and partly clad in stone with cedar shingles on the roof.

These projects were designed and supervised by architects Messrs Marsh & Waite of Kings Lynn who have been involved in the Royal Estate and the visitor centre since the supply of the first building.

The next project was to take place in 1977 when Colt supplied a wet weather shelter adjacent to the cafeteria. The building was open sided with a shingled roof supported on 10 timber cedar clad columns. This was designed for visitors to shelter during inclement weather before visiting the cafeteria, which since it had been built, had become popular with visitors to the estate. Generally for these projects, a local building company formed the foundations while the timber structure itself was being manufactured in the Colt factory. Working as a sub-contractor to Colt, Terry Tierney carried out the erection and completion of this building on site. This was the first of the Sandringham projects to be carried out by Terry whose long association began in 1972 and who purchased the company in 1996.

The souvenir shop

Ranger's and First Aid Room

The wet weather shelter before the glass infill

The wet weather shelter as a tea room with windows

The link to the original cafeteria

The restaurant under construction

In 1982 the addition of a ranger's and first aid room was built close to the souvenir shop. A new entrance to the shop was fitted and a link fence to the ranger's room was erected. Also as part of this project, the octagonal flower stall was extended.

In 1984, the wet weather shelter was converted to become part of the cafeteria by filling in the walls. This was achieved by fitting panels between the timber columns. The panels had large windows making the building very light. To complete its link to the cafeteria, a transit shelter was built connecting the shelter to the original cafeteria building. This was for food being bought in the cafeteria. In 1989 a larger cafeteria was built which also housed a new kitchen, allowing the original cafeteria to be used for more seating. This extension made the new area over three times that of the original cafeteria supplied in 1969. This had elevated the status to restaurant while the building which was originally the wet weather shelter was used as a tea room. Only four years later work started on a purpose built kitchen adjacent to the restaurant. The new complex which was opened in 1994 boasted seating for 200 for informal dining, 230 for banquets and 500 for buffet functions.

The completed restaurant showing the Prince of Wales feathers on the wall. These were salvaged from a Sandringham house demolished some twenty years earlier

The purpose built kitchen building shown with the link to the restaurant

During the last project, a walkway around the souvenir shop was supplied by W H Colt to allow expansion of the shop sales area

A clever "Artist's Impression" of the centre by Desmond Waite which shows most of the complex including, in the centre of the picture, the original 1969 W H Colt building

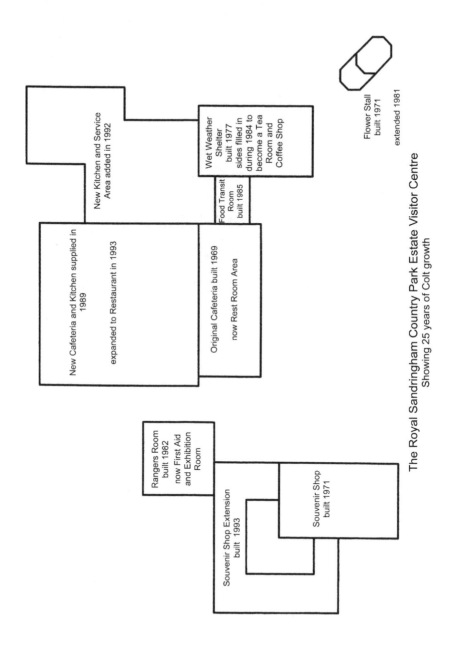

New Kitchen and Service Area added in 1992

New Cafeteria and Kitchen supplied in 1989

expanded to Restaurant in 1993

Wet Weather Shelter built 1977 sides filled in during 1984 to become a Tea Room and Coffee Shop

Food Transit Room built 1985

Original Cafeteria built 1969

now Rest Room Area

Flower Stall built 1971

extended 1981

Rangers Room built 1982 now First Aid and Exhibition Room

Souvenir Shop Extension built 1993

Souvenir Shop built 1971

The Royal Sandringham Country Park Estate Visitor Centre
Showing 25 years of Colt growth

Desmond Waite of Marsh & Waite ensured that all the new additions carried out through the years always complimented those existing and his designs were meticulous in every detail. During this final project he maintained overall direction and control. He was responsible for conception, construction and quality and scope of on-site works.

The construction program was tight and using the Colt system of manufacturing the building in their factory at Bethersden while the site was prepared for the arrival of the building was a contributing factor in ensuring that the project was delivered on time and on budget.

W H Colts long association with this project earned the company the Royal Seal of approval by becoming "by appointment to her Majesty the Queen supplier of pre-fabricated timber framed houses and structures".

The Visitor Centre at Sandringham is a tribute to the dedication of all those involved at W H Colt who made the project a success.

Author's Note:

The following pages were kindly donated by Mr Desmond Waite who was the principal architect involved with development of the visitor centre. Here he describes the design sequence of the buildings which were to be supplied by W H Colt.

I would express my gratitude for this contribution which I am sure readers will find interesting.

Clive Kennett

The Sandringham Visitor Centre: Design Review

By the architect: Desmond K. Waite MVO F.R.I.B.A.

Having been Consultant Architect for the Queen at her Sandringham Estate (but not the house) from early 1960s I became responsible for the design of the visitor centre complex. Before my time, it all started with a timber shed with flap up hatch to supply refreshments for visitors, set within the present site but replaced by the Colt constructed cafeteria due to increasing demand. Ticket access to the gardens was also under pressure.

I designed the ticket office set straddling the perimeter wall of Sandringham House garden using traditional materials, followed quickly by the first basic yet popular souvenir shop. That shop was achieved with the timber structure built by W. H. Colt to my design from Colt standard panels and roof covering of plain shingles with some wall texture of local Carr stone. However, the absence of adequate indoor cafeteria space for visitors became a problem in bad weather. I was asked to design and arrange for a protected open shelter.

The Wet Shelter

W H Colt responded again to my design for an unusual tent like image of a roof on stilts with cedar clad steel posts and a large overhang to bring the eaves into scale. The building was a success but the paving slab floor deck with bench seat tables suffered with food and drink staining not regularly washed by the rain.

With visitor numbers increasing it was agreed that the wet shelter would be enclosed to become a tea room with its own small kitchen and dedicated separate manageress. The burden of success caused some difficulties in kitchen services and I designed a new link superstructure between the kitchens, integrating with roof junctions and shapes but increasingly, visitors seeking refreshments suffered in bad weather especially when seeking the slightly remote lavatory blocks serving the Country Park.

The Complex with a Restaurant

I was called in to the Sandringham Estate Office in 1990 and briefed to think about and produce a sketch design for an extension to integrate all buildings and provide a restaurant for 200 people with dedicated toilets all in a master plan overall for future options.

I felt that I had a free hand but I knew that the Keeper of the Privy Purse was relying upon the general Estate Manager for cost control and profit-ability and that a budget with the design had to be approved by Her Majesty. I worked up a costing for a budget figure in the pre-assessment for the building design which was subsequently approved.

The Design

By now my son Richard was qualified within our practice and we re-solved that the new building ought not to be architecture in conflict with the park like setting. I knew that there was scepticism about its need thus the building had to be convincing yet grand enough to be special, using materials from nature.

The souvenir shop joined with a pyramid roofed ranger's room was set to mark the entrance to the whole complex for pedestrians approaching from large new coach and car parks. The shop was rearranged using the existing shape in matching materials with its doubled size under a gently sloping flat roofed area softened by stained green boards capping dia-mond shaped well spaced small display windows to allow wall space inter-nally and to offer unique expectation for visitors walking in from the other car parks.

The large restaurant bulk had to avoid fashionable funny roof shapes and

67

be in scale at domestic level or the mass itself would be in conflict. Natural materials with lasting qualities would be relatively low in maintenance costs if left to weather. W.H. Colt were thus able to agree Western Red cedar cladding boards, cedar shakes for an impressive textured roof cladding and cultivated (not rain forest) Douglas Fir window and door joinery to suit this criteria. The building became timber framed with standard Colt wall panels fabricated off site as were the Glulam shaped portal roof frames featured   internally.

Making use of the existing cafeteria for the restaurant lavatories and its roof void and tower like ventilation shaft for air conditioning plant, enabled the large building to integrate. The vast new kitchen area had to be flat roofed but screened behind pitched parapet edges, linking with other pitched roofs to create a homogeneous composition of different massing in building shapes embracing the popular outside space for visitors to gather.

The design was approved subject to costs, incorporating a new feature building for flowers plus ice cream and the first aid facilities. The way was clear to invite expertise from W. H. Colt known to me to have perfectionist attitudes, to consider costs in supplying and fixing of timberwork in the   superstructure, working with similarly motivated   local building contractor, Gilbert Construction, to offer costings for co-ordinating other trades and specialists.

The striking and completed visitor centre was opened by Her Majesty the Queen in 1994. The quality of the building under my direction could not have been achieved without the courage of the Estate Manager and the indulgence of the Keeper of the Privy Purse. It also needed the dedicated fabrication team from W. H. Colt and their Terry Tierny construction teams who worked all daylight hours whilst living on site joining with the skills assembled by the main contractor Richard Gilbert. All participants   entered   into the spirit of perfection expected.

Desmond K. Waite MVO F.R.I.B.A .

Changing Work - 1990 to 2000

Despite a falling order book during the nineties, buildings were still being produced by Colt, although the trend toward commercial rather than residential continued.

Also, given the number of Colt houses that had been supplied over the years, there was a growing demand for refurbishment of roof and wall cladding, as well as for extensions and this work kept the factory going.

Yet another example of a commercial project undertaken by the company in this period is the Hennerton Golf Club in Berkshire where a new clubhouse was supplied for a brand new golf course. With less new build houses being supplied, the company continued to offer extension and renovation services to the occupiers of Colt Houses and this has continued alongside new build.

Built in 1992, the building was featured in the Golf Club handbook

Despite the low number of residential buildings which were under-taken by the company at this time, there remained some major projects which the company undertook. One of these being the club house for Faversham Golf Club which is a fine example of a modern building built with a very traditional look. This building was completed in 1997.

Generally during this period, the company continued to run down although the company records show that extensions and additions to existing homes were being carried out. From a commercial point of view nothing had been done to bring standard designs up to date or introduce new catalogues but the company continued to operate from the factory and offices in Bethersden. In 1996, W H Colt Son & Co Ltd was purchased by Terry Tierney. Terry had spent many years carrying out ground work and erecting the houses as a sub-contractor to Colt and he took the opportunity to

Gillingham Golf Club in Kent where the whole first floor was supplied and erected by W H Colt Son & Company Ltd

Faversham Golf Club

take it on when those running it decided to retire. Operations continued for a further four years in Bethersden until in 2000 manufacturing was moved to Challock in Kent. The show houses in Bethersden remain in the ownership of Colt Estates but are now privately let.

Modern Times - 2000 & Beyond

With less land being available for individual house construction, the requirement for new build for that market has decreased but the company continues to find work in renovating and extending existing Colt homes. Drawings of houses supplied over the years have been retained, thus making extension and renovation possible by having reference to the original drawings. Also, where windows have deteriorated, it is possible from the drawings to supply new windows direct to current owners to have fitted themselves or the company can offer a fitting service. Quotations can normally be supplied without on-site measuring such is the accuracy of the original manufacture and the information retained by the company. Modern windows tend to be uPVC or aluminium and replace the original Crittal metal frame windows which were supplied with the Colt houses.

Colt house owners are enthusiastic about living in their homes and are keen to preserve them and improve them which means that today the Colt phone is seldom quiet. The company generally offers a number of improvements for Colt houses. This can range from straight forward window replacement and cedar roof and wall shingle renewal, to the insulating of walls and loft space and the building of extensions.

Extensions can mean simply adding an extra room to a bungalow but occasionally more ambitious projects are carried whereby a roof is lifted or replaced on a bungalow to add a first floor. The company currently carries out some ambitious extensions which achieve not only an increase in the footprint of a house, but also where planners and space permits, an increase in the height. It is often possible to carry out the upward extensions without the need for the occupants to move out during the alterations. This is typical of the work currently carried out by modern day Colt Houses.

Typical Project

The following is an example of an upward extension where a first floor is added to a bungalow.

Before the upwards extension

After - believe it or not - a first floor is added!

Another Project

Another major renovation project which was carried out in 2005 by the company was that of a house near Canterbury in Kent. Originally built in 1923 it had become run down having not been maintained for many years. New owners were urged by friends to demolish the house and start afresh, but they were persuaded that the character of the house would be maintained by renovation and they chose Colt Houses to carry out those renovations.

The oldest photograph of the house near Canterbury

The following photograph appeared in an early Colt Catalogue dated 1938 The catalogue states that the approximate all in cost for this house, excluding the central heating, was £975. However in the catalogue, the price has been crossed out in pen and a revised price of £1085 written in along with the words *"(in Kent)."*

The house as it appeared in a thirties catalogue

The sad state of the house after years of neglect and before Colt started its work

As part of the renovation project, all external cladding was removed, the walls insulated and the cladding replaced. The original lean-to had already disappeared. The house was fitted with new timber cladding to the first floor elevations and render to the ground floor. A new kitchen extension was added to the rear which was given an external skin of brickwork. When the original cladding was removed, the timber frame of the house was found to be in near perfect condition.

The front elevation after completion of phase one of the renovation

The side elevation showing the kitchen extension

Two years later a Colt sun room is added

Another example of a less ambitious project is shown above whereby external cedar shingles have been replaced and a new oriel window fitted

For almost 100 years of operation, and of mixed fortunes, Colt Houses continues to thrive. Not at the same levels as were seen in the sixties and seventies, but the name of Colt lives on and within the vast stock of some 16000 houses which have been supplied over the years live a group of people who are proud to be part of this story.

Technical Details

During the near century in which the company has been manufacturing, there have been a number of changes in the manufacturing methods. This has been for various reasons over this time. Availability of materials and requirements of building regulations have influenced the way in which the houses have been manufactured.

Cedar has been a constant factor and the company has always emphasised the fact that the red cedar (Thuya Plicata) is used for roofs and cladding. It is often called Arbor Vitae meaning the tree of life and the timber used for construction purposes is grown in British Columbia. The timber is reputed to be distasteful to insects and vermin and is highly resistant to rot. The timber has also been shown to be immune to dry rot fungus.

For these reasons the timber is highly suitable for tiles, cladding and external trims as it does not require treatment with paint or preservatives, thus keeping maintenance costs down. With no treatment, it is said that the cedar tiles and cladding will last over 20 years. Experience has shown that the timber has lasted much longer in some cases. On new houses today and on houses that are re-clad, the shingles are pressure treated with preservative and require no further treatment for 25 years following which it is recommended to apply a preservative at five year intervals. The cedar cladding supplied, remains un-treated but a cedar oil - Texnap 22 - is supplied with all structures delivered.

Originally when Colt was manufacturing poultry houses the modular system was used whereby completed panels were created to keep costs down. However, in the early years of house construction the modular approach was deemed less appropriate and from the early twenties, houses were being "stick built" on site from random lengths of 4" x 2" (100mm x 50mm). Stick built refers to the method of making up panels on site rather than them being manufactured in a factory. This method continued until the war years.

Following the war, the company returned to the manufacturing of modular panels but due to timber shortages at this time, the size of the timber used in construction was reduced to $1^1/_4$" x $2^3/_4$" (32mm x 70mm). In this case the panels were not load bearing. The vertical load was borne by a stanchion at the junction of each panel. Also for a short time in the early fifties aluminium stanchions or vertical members (shown in the cross section below) were used between the panels as the load bearing member. This was possibly due to the ready supply of aluminium after the war and the shortage of timber. The aluminium stanchions were not used for very long before being replaced by Maranti (hardwood) stanchions which measured $4^3/_4$" x $1^1/_4$" (121mm x 32mm). This was after recommendation by the ministry of works. (Nowadays, we have the building control office.)

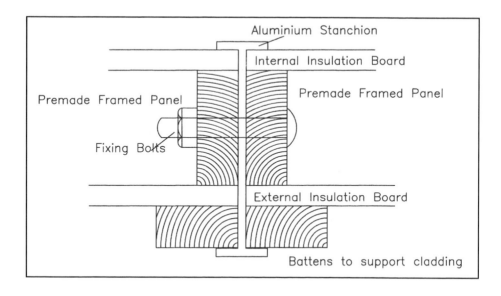

A cross section through a wall showing the aluminium stanchion. This method was used between 1948 and 1952

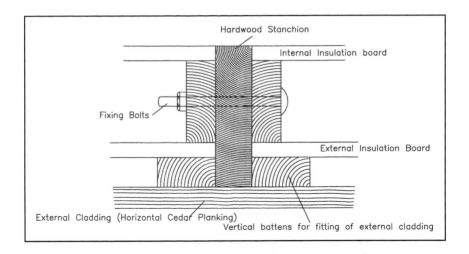

This cross section shows the hardwood stanchion. This method was
introduced in the early fifties and was used for about 10 years

Some archive drawings from the late forties showed the occa-
sional use of steel stanchions where a particular load bearing ca-
pacity was required.

The modular panels were always based on a nominal 4' width to
accommodate the standard 8' x 4' (2438mm x 1216mm) insulation
board. The actual manufacturing width of the panel was changed
slightly as the different type of stanchions were introduced, thus
maintaining the 4' between centres.

During the early days of the modular approach, the floor panels
for the first floor were also modular. These were nominally 4'
square to be supported by the primary and secondary support
beams which form the grid into which the floor panels sit. This is
shown quite well in an extract from "The Architect & Building
News" which featured a house designed by a Mr A L Osborne.
The article is dated 25th February 1949.

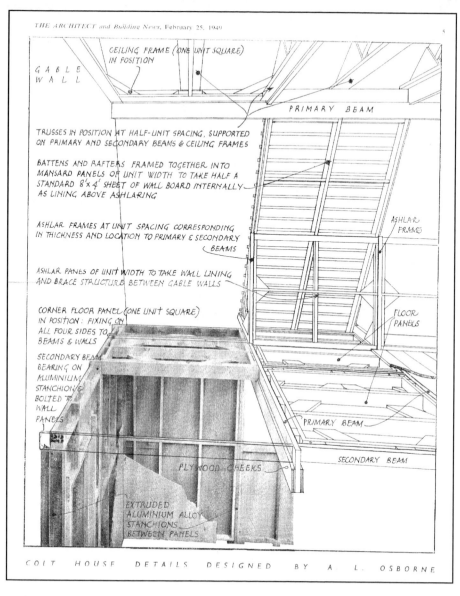

GABLE
WALL

CEILING FRAME (ONE UNIT SQUARE)
IN POSITION

PRIMARY BEAM

TRUSSES IN POSITION AT HALF-UNIT SPACING, SUPPORTED
ON PRIMARY AND SECONDARY BEAMS & CEILING FRAMES

BATTENS AND RAFTERS FRAMED TOGETHER INTO
MANSARD PANELS OF UNIT WIDTH TO TAKE HALF A
STANDARD 8'x 4' SHEET OF WALL BOARD INTERNALLY
AS LINING ABOVE ASHLARING

ASHLAR FRAMES AT UNIT SPACING CORRESPONDING
IN THICKNESS AND LOCATION TO PRIMARY & SECONDARY
BEAMS

ASHLAR PANES OF UNIT WIDTH TO TAKE WALL LINING
AND BRACE STRUCTURE BETWEEN GABLE WALLS

CORNER FLOOR PANEL (ONE UNIT SQUARE)
IN POSITION : FIXING ON
ALL FOUR SIDES TO
BEAMS & WALLS

SECONDARY BEAM
BEARING ON
ALUMINIUM
STANCHIONS
BOLTED TO
WALL
PANELS

ASHLAR
FRAMES

FLOOR
PANELS

PRIMARY BEAM

SECONDARY BEAM

PLYWOOD CHEEKS

EXTRUDED
ALUMINIUM ALLOY
STANCHIONS
BETWEEN PANELS

COIT HOUSE DETAILS DESIGNED BY A. L. OSBORNE

The above extract was used in a 1953 catalogue with a foot note:

"The aluminium and plywood shown have now been replaced by imported hardwood as recommended by M.O.W." (Ministry of Works)

During the sixties, the more conventional method of using joists for first floor construction was employed. Over the next few years the construction methods were changed to reflect material availability and mass production. Internal insulation board was replaced by the more modern plasterboard which gives a much better internal finish to the houses. Externally however the houses continued to be clad in either cedar shingles of horizontal cedar boarding as they have been for many years.

The sketch below shows the configuration of these panels and the machined softwood stanchion which was the load bearing member. This method remained in use until the nineties.

The components of the house were built to precision and today the company retains drawings of every Colt house ever built. If the current occupier of a Colt home requires replacement windows, these can be supplied from dimensions given on the drawings without the need to re-measure on site.

Having these accurate records also means that a property can be

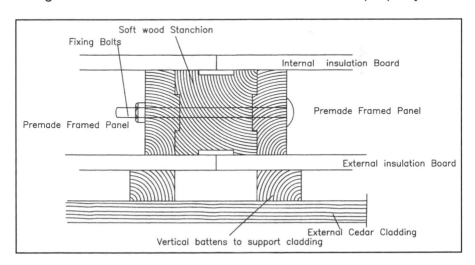

The softwood stanchion was introduced in the sixties and remained in use for over thirty years

extended giving reference to the original drawings. It is also possible to extend upwards by removing the roof and adding an extra floor as has been shown.

To reflect the increasing need for more insulation and available materials, in modern Colt houses the frames are manufactured from CLS (Canadian Lumber Stock) in either 90mm or 140mm thick panels. To achieve today's building regulation requirements for energy saving it is normal to use 140mm panels. The panels are designed as load bearing and eliminating the need for stanchions between the panels. This means that the method of construction has once again moved away from the "4 foot" panel. With modern methods of mechanical handling however it is possible to manufacture much larger panels but this means that no longer can a Colt house be built by a carpenter and his boy.

Also, as it is often pointed out in Colt catalogues, a further advantage of using the timber frame method of construction is that the house, having been built using no wet trades, is completely dry from completion of construction. 100 years ago, conventionally built houses were left unoccupied for a year to dry out.

Colt and Cedar Construction were for many years registered as NHB(R)C builders and would carry out all the works, from drawings and planning applications to local authorities to completing the house ready for moving in.

A modern Colt building under construction (Buckmore Park ambulance station in Kent)

An external view of Buckmore Park ambulance station in Kent

Conclusions

Without a doubt, William Colt was a pioneer in building the popularity of the timber house. Without his innovation and drive, we may not have a timber frame industry in Britain as we have today. Despite the scepticism of the British house buyer and builder, timber frame construction has become more popular over the last several decades and much of this is down to the Colt House.

Despite all the information available in respect of Colt products over the years, there is very little information about William Colt himself who appears to have been a very private man. When Jack O'Hea was pushing the company forward, Mr Colt stayed out of the limelight and continued to innovate and build houses. It was Jack who went to the exhibitions and Jack who showed the Prince of Wales around the demonstration Miners' Cottage in London.

William Colt's son Michael also played his part in moving the family business forward. Following his father's death in 1945 at a comparatively young age, Michael was instrumental in building the business in the years following the war. He remained dedicated to the company and its products until his own death in 1985.

To date, Colt has supplied over 16,000 buildings to all parts of the UK and the world. They range from the early poultry houses and simple workman's cottages through to manor houses, old peoples homes, schools, offices, golf club houses and many more, all designed with style and manufactured with care. The company's unique products continue to be held in high esteem. Colt was probably the first commercial timber frame company in existence in England although many have appeared (and disappeared) since. Colt owners are proud to be so and are willing to show their house to others. Unfortunately, some of these houses have gone but the vast majority remain carrying the Colt name forward.

Within this book, we have endeavoured to show designs and styles of houses through the decades and the range is extensive and while tastes and fashions change it is clear that many of the Colt designs introduced in the twenties and thirties are as viable today as practical homes as they were when they were first introduced.

As W H Colt Son & Co Ltd heads for the end of its first hundred years and its centenary celebrations, who knows what the future holds for the company and indeed the industry.

Three more satisfied customers

From the back of the seventies catalogues.........

Further reading—"The Sky's the Limit" by Nigel Watson—The story of how Jack O'Hea went on to build the other Colt organisation.